故園畫憶

庚寅中秋 韓磬陸題

《故园画忆系列》编委会

名誉主任：韩启德

主　　任：邵　鸿

委　　员：（按姓氏笔画为序）

万　捷	王秋桂	方李莉	叶培贵
刘魁立	况　晗	严绍璗	吴为山
范贻光	范　芳	孟　白	邵　鸿
岳庆平	郑培凯	唐晓峰	曹兵武

故园画忆系列
Memory of the Old
Home in Sketches

济南老风情
Ji'nan in its Good Old Days

周迎峰 绘画 撰文
Sketches & Notes by Zhou Yingfeng

学苑出版社
Academy Press

图书在版编目（CIP）数据

济南老风情 / 周迎峰绘画、撰文. — 北京：学苑出版社，2015.9

（故园画忆系列）

ISBN 978-7-5077-4846-8

Ⅰ. ①济… Ⅱ. ①周… Ⅲ. ①钢笔画—作品集—中国—现代 ②古建筑—介绍—济南市 ③风俗习惯—介绍—济南市 Ⅳ. ①J224 ②K928.71 ③K892.452.1

中国版本图书馆CIP数据核字（2015）第206684号

出 版 人：	孟　白
责任编辑：	周　鼎
编　　辑：	何纯谱
出版发行：	学苑出版社
社　　址：	北京市丰台区南方庄2号院1号楼
邮政编码：	100079
网　　址：	www.book001.com
电子信箱：	xueyuanpress@163.com
销售电话：	010-67601101（营销部）、67603091（总编室）
经　　销：	全国新华书店
印 刷 厂：	北京信彩瑞禾印刷厂
开本尺寸：	889×1194　1/24
印　　张：	5.75
字　　数：	140千字
图　　幅：	120幅
版　　次：	2015年9月北京第1版
印　　次：	2015年9月北京第1次印刷
定　　价：	42.00元

目　录

自序　　　　　　　　　　周迎峰

历史建筑

趵突泉·观澜亭	3
趵突泉·望鹤亭	4
趵突泉·泺源堂	5
趵突泉·娥英祠	6
趵突泉·白雪楼	7
趵突泉·三圣殿	8
趵突泉·万竹园	9
趵突泉·李清照纪念堂	10
大明湖·历下亭	11
大明湖·北极阁	12
大明湖·汇波楼	13
大明湖·铁公祠	14
大明湖·小沧浪亭	15
大明湖·牌坊	16
灵岩寺·辟支塔	17
灵岩寺·千佛殿	18
灵岩寺·千佛殿彩塑	19
灵岩寺·大雄宝殿	20
灵岩寺·墓塔林	21
灵岩寺·慧崇塔	22
灵岩寺·天王殿	23
灵岩寺·鼓楼	24
灵岩寺·钟楼	25
府学文庙	26
济南清真南大寺	27
济南清真北大寺	28
兴福寺	29
长春观	30
清巡抚院署	31
升阳观	32
永济桥	33
四门塔	34
九顶塔	35
百脉泉	36
黑虎泉	37
珍珠泉	38
五龙潭	39
千佛山	40
红叶谷	41
九如山	42
曲水亭街	43
上新街	44
芙蓉街	45

所里街	46	齐鲁大学·办公楼	72
章丘朱家峪·文昌阁	47	齐鲁大学·考文楼	73
章丘朱家峪·祠堂	48	齐鲁大学·柏根楼	74
章丘朱家峪·康熙立交桥	49	齐鲁大学医学院·共合楼	75
		齐鲁大学医学院·求真楼	76
近代建筑		齐鲁大学医学院·新兴楼	77
将军庙天主教堂	53	济南懿范女子中学	78
洪家楼天主教堂	54	广智院	79
林家庄天主教堂	55	同仁会济南医院	80
陈家楼天主教堂	56	山东红卍字会施诊所	81
英国浸礼会礼拜堂	57	解放阁	82
后宰门街基督教礼拜堂	58	跳伞塔	83
济南德国领事馆	59	宏济堂	84
济南日本总领事馆	60	山东省实验中学老校门	85
济南美国领事馆	61	山东省济南第一中学旧址	86
济南老火车站	62	金氏公馆	87
黄台车站	63	老舍旧居	88
津浦铁路洛口黄河大桥	64	泉城广场	89
济南府电报收发局	65		
瑞蚨祥布店	66	**民俗文化**	
英美烟草公司	67	山东吕剧	93
丰大洋行	68	山东皮影	94
德华银行济南分行旧址	69	山东琴书	95
济南交通银行大厦	70	山东大鼓	96
山东大学堂	71	山东快书	97

山东木板大鼓	98	济南泥塑	114
五音戏	99	济南剪纸	115
平阴木偶戏	100	侯氏社火脸谱	116
柳子戏	101	葫芦雕刻	117
商河鼓子秧歌	102	周氏兔子王	118
济南相声	103	绣球灯	119
高跷"乔家"	104	章丘铁匠	120
章丘龙舞	105	千佛山庙会	121
阿胶制作工艺	106	宏济堂传统中药	122
济南油旋制作工艺	107	大观园晨光茶社	123
龙山黑陶制作技艺	108	明湖采藕	124
商河老粗布制作技艺	109	放河灯	125
玉谦旗袍制作技艺	110	章丘芯子	126
崮山馍馍制作技艺	111	形意拳	127
鲁绣	112	太平拳	128
济南面塑	113		

Contents

Preface   Zhou Yingfeng

Historic Architecture

Sprouting Spring • Guanlan Pavilion	3
Sprouting Spring • Wanghe Pavillion	4
Sprouting Spring • Luoyuan Hall	5
Sprouting Spring • E'ying Ancestral Temple	6
Sprouting Spring • Baixue Hall	7
Sprouting Spring • Sansheng Hall	8
Sprouting Spring • Wanzhu Garden	9
Sprouting Spring • Li Qingzhao Memorial Hall	10
Daming Lake • Lixia Pavilion	11
Daming Lake • Beiji Pavillion	12
Daming Lake • Huibo Tower	13
Daming Lake • Tiegong Ancestral Temple	14
Daming Lake • Little Canglang	15
Daming Lake • Memorial Archway	16
Lingyan Temple • Pizhi Tower	17
Lingyan Temple • Qianfo Hall	18
Lingyan Temple • Colored Sculptures in Qianfo Hall	19
Lingyan Temple • Mahavira Hall	20
Lingyan Temple • Tomb Pagoda Forest	21
Lingyan Temple • Huichong Tower	22
Lingyan Temple • Hall of Heavenly Kings	23
Lingyan Temple • Drum Tower	24
Lingyan Temple • Bell Tower	25
Fuxue Confucian Temple	26
The North Mosque	27
The South Mosque	28
Xingfu Temple	29
Changchun Taoist Temple	30
Shandong Governor's Compound of Qing Dynasty	31
Shengyang Taoist Temple	32
Yongji Bridge	33
Simen Pagoda	34
Jiuding Tower	35
Baimai Spring	36
Heihu Spring (Black Tiger Spring)	37
Pearl Spring	38
Wulong Pool (Five-Dragon Pool)	39
Mount Qianfo	40
Hongye Valley	41
Jiuru Mountain	42
Qushuiting Street	43
Shangxin Street	44
Furong Street	45

Suoli Street	46	British American Tobacco China	67
Zhangqiu Zhujiayu Village • Wenchang Pavilion	47	Fengda Foreign Bank	68
Zhangqiu Zhujiayu Village • The Zhu's Ancestral Memorial	48	Former Site of the Ji'nan Branch of Deutsche Asiatische Bank	69
Zhangqiu Zhujiayu Village • Kangxi Overpasses	49	Ji'nan Bank of Communications	70
		Shandong Imperial University	71
		Cheeloo University • Office Building	72
		Cheeloo University • Mateer Hall	73

Modern Architecture

Jiangjunmiao Catholic Church	53	Cheeloo University • Bergen Hall	74
Hongjialou Catholic Church	54	Cheeloo University Medical School • Gonghe Building	75
Linjiazhuang Catholic Church	55	Cheeloo University Medical School • Qiuzhen Building	76
Chenjialou Catholic Church	56	Cheeloo University Medical School • Xinxing Building	77
British Baptist Church	57	Ji'nan Yifan Middle School for Girls	78
Houzaimen Christian Church	58	Guangzhiyuan Museum	79
Original Site of German Consulate to Ji'nan	59	Tongrenhui Ji'nan Hospital Main Building	80
Original Site of Japanese Consulate to Ji'nan	60	The Red Swastika Society Clinic of Shandong Province	81
Original Site of American Consulate to Ji'nan	61	Jiefang Pavilion	82
Old Ji'nan Railway Station	62	Skydiving Tower	83
Huangtai Railway Station	63	Hongjitang Museum	84
Tiensin-Pukow Railway Luokou Bridge over the Yellow River	64	The Old Gate of Shandong	
Ji'nan Municipal Telegraph Bureau	65		
Ruifuxiang Cloth Store	66		

Experimental High School	85	Ji'nan Youxuan Making Technic	107
The Original Site of Ji'nan No. 1 High School	86	Longshan Black Pottery Craftsmanship	108
		Shanghe Handwoven Cloth Craftsmanship	109
The Jin's Residence	87	Yuqian Cheongsam Craftsmanship	110
Laoshe Memorial	88	Gushan Steamed Bun Craftsmanship	111
Spring City Square	89	Lu Embroidery	112
		Ji'nan Dough Modeling	113
Folk Arts		Ji'nan Clay Figuring	114
Shangdong Lü Opera	93	Ji'nan Papercutting	115
Shandong Leather Silhouettes Show	94	The Hou's Club Fire Facial Mask	116
Shandong Qinshu	95	Calabash Engraving	117
Shandong Drum	96	The Zhou's Rabbit Clay Figuring	118
Shandong Clapper Ballad	97	Silk Ball Lantern Dance	119
Shandong Wood Plate Drum	98	Blacksmith in Zhangqiu	120
Five-tone Drama	99	Temple Fair on Mount Qianfo	121
Pingyin Puppet Show	100	Hongjitang Traditional Chinese Medicine	122
Liuzi Opera	101	Chenguang Tea House in Daguanyuan Mall	123
Shanghe Drum Yangko Dance	102	Lotus Root Harvest in Daming Lake	124
Ji'nan Cross-talk	103	Floating River Lanterns	125
The Qiao's Stilts Dance	104	Zhangqiu Xinzi	126
Zhangqiu Dragon Dance	105	Xingyi Chinese Boxing	127
Donkey-hide Gelatin Craftsmanship	106	Taiping Chinese Boxing	128

自 序

济南，又称泉城。济南泉水众多，比较著名的就有72个，其中，天下第一泉——趵突泉最负盛名。济南的泉个个皆有故事和传说，充满了灵性。"四面荷花三面柳，一城山色半城湖"，这是诗人的赞誉，更是老济南人的集体记忆。有多少人是看过了老舍先生的《济南的冬天》而对济南这座城市心向往之的？又有多少人是读过了李易安的"兴尽晚回舟，误入藕花深处"而想走进济南的深处，去看看孕育了这个千古女词人的历城究竟是一座怎样的城的？正如老舍先生说"济南的冬天是响晴的"，我也想说，济南这座城市也是温情的。

悠悠泉水，青青山脉，承载的岂止是千百年的历史和文化？她也沧桑，沧桑得可以追溯到大舜躬耕的时代；她也霸气，霸气得让人想到唐初辅佐李世民打下江山的大将秦琼；她也神秘，文武双全的辛弃疾如同这个城市的性格，让人于蓦然回首处，方才领略她的韵味与风情。还有享誉全国的瑞蚨祥，又让人想到了她的另一面——热闹和繁华。如果把这个城市比作女子，定是秀外慧中、美貌与智慧兼备的那一款吧？难怪有人把济南比作北方的小江南。

感谢学苑出版社的"故园画忆"项目，让我有机会拿起画笔，把济南的历史建筑、名胜古迹、风俗人情用速写的形式呈现出来。一年多来我走遍了济南的大街小巷，去探寻、去聆听，去用心感受这个城市的细碎点滴，去想象这个城市失落了的往昔。因此，对我来说，这本书不仅仅是一本艺术图集，更是我用手中的笔在描绘一座心中的城。

整体来看，本书的120幅图主要描绘了三个部分：历史建筑、近代建筑、民俗文化。绘画的过程，对我是一种心灵的洗礼。每一个线条都包含了我对传统文化的尊重和热爱。

在此，还要特别感谢学苑出版社周鼎老师给我提供了这样一次宝贵的机会，允许我大胆地用自己的方式将"老济南"呈现给读者。感谢山东师范大学美术学院的张望院长在百忙之中为本书作序。由于本人才疏学浅，作品中疏漏在所难免，还望大家批评指教。

周迎峰

2015年2月

Preface

Ji'nan is also known as the Spring City for the numerous springs scattered around the city. The most famous one, among the 72 widely-known springs, is Spouting Spring. but each spring has its own story.

There is a significant amount of Chinese literature paying tribute to the beautiful landscapes in Ji'nan. This entices many tourists to visit Ji'nan. Lao She (1899-1966), a famous Chinese writer, wrote that Ji'nan's winter is tender. So is the city.

The springs and mountains carry a history of thousands of years. The city is old and mysterious on one hand while lively and prosperous on the other. If it were to be compared to a woman, she must be beautiful in her appearance and wise in her mind. It is no wonder that Ji'nan sometimes is called "Little Jiangnan (the lower reaches of the Yangtze River)".

I am thankful to the *Memory of the Old Home in Sketches* program sponsored by the Academy Press, which gives me an opportunity to paint the historic architecture, tourist attractions, and old customs in Ji'nan with a realistic touch. For me, this book is more than an album of paintings. It is a depiction of the city in my heart created with my own hands.

This album consists of three parts: Historic Architecture, Modern Architecture and Folk Arts. 120 paintings record the landscape, historical sites, culture and customs of Ji'nan. The creative process is a one of rediscovery for me. Each and every line is full with respect and love for the traditional Chinese culture.

I am especially grateful to Mr. Zhou Ding from the Academy Press who has given me this precious opportunity that allows me to present the old Ji'nan to the readers in my own way.

Zhou Yingfeng
February, 2015

历史建筑
Historic Architecture

趵突泉·观澜亭

位于历下区趵突泉西侧，建于明天顺五年（1461年）。亭子建于高台之上，泉水之中，是观赏趵突泉水的最佳之处。该亭原为四面长亭、半封闭式，现改为四面敞亭。

Sprouting Spring • Guanlan Pavilion

Built in 1461 on a high platform to the west of the Sprouting Spring, Guanlan Pavilion is an open booth converted from the original one which was half enclosed. It is the best spot to appreciate the Sprouting Spring.

[趵突泉·望鹤亭]

　　位于趵突泉东北隅，原称"漱玉亭"，清代乾隆年间（1736～1795年）更名为"望鹤亭"。该亭呈丁字形，为卷棚悬山建筑，小青瓦面，琉璃门窗，东西两间中部南侧，辟有圆形洞门，门外隙地，植垂柳，依柳叠山石。

Sprouting Spring • Wanghe Pavillion
Located northeast of the Sprouting Spring, Wanghe Pavillion was changed to its current name from the original "Suyü Pavillion" during the reign of the Qing Emperor, Qianlong (1736-1795).

趵突泉·泺源堂

位于趵突泉北岸,著名文学家曾巩在宋熙宁年间(1068～1077年)所建,因其临泺水的源头,故称"泺源堂"。殿前为卷棚式厦檐,楣额透雕云纹、彩亭、禽兽、花卉等图案,显得玲珑古典。今存殿堂三座,坐北朝南,建在同一中轴线上,是一组较大的明清建筑。

Sprouting Spring • Luoyuan Hall

The famous writer, Zeng Gong, built Luoyuan Hall on the north bank of the Sprouting Spring during the Xi'ning reign period (1068-1077) of North Song Emperor Zhao Xu. The existing three buildings are on the central axis facing south. They form a large complex of buildings.

趵突泉·娥英祠

　　为位于泺源堂北面的明代建筑，祭祀舜之二妃娥皇、女英，是泺源堂的著名景点。

Sprouting Spring • E'ying Ancestral Temple

This is a building from the Ming Dynasty (1368-1644). It sits to the north of Luoyuan Hall in memory of E'huang and Nüying, two concubines of the legendary and ancient Emperor Shun.

趵突泉·白雪楼

位于趵突泉的东南侧，为纪念明代文学后七子领袖李攀龙而建。正厅内陈放着李攀龙全身坐姿铜像，有其弟子学生及当代名人所题写篆刻的诗文匾额，再现了当年李攀龙先生诗词的盛景。

Sprouting Spring • Baixue Hall

Baixue Hall was built on the southeast side of the Sprouting Spring in memory of Li Panlong, the leader of 7 elites of literature during the late Ming Dynasty (1368-1644). A copper statue of Li Panlong sits in the main hall alongside inscribed boards of poems and essays by his students and modern celebrities.

【趵突泉·三圣殿】

　　位于趵突泉北岸，始建于明代。因其纪念尧、舜、禹三圣而称三圣殿。现殿内供奉尧、舜、禹和四大臣的塑像。

Sprouting Spring • Sansheng Hall

Sansheng Hall was built in the Ming Dynasty on the north bank of the Sprouting Spring in memory of the three sages, Emperor Yao, Shun and Yu. Statues of these sages and four ministers of Emperor Yao are enshrined inside.

趵突泉·万竹园

　　位于趵突泉公园西侧，始建于元代，因园中多竹而得名。曾是山东督军张怀芝的私家花园，又名张家花园，占地面积1.2万多平方米，该园有三套院落，13个庭院，186间房屋，还有五桥、四亭、一花园及望水泉、东高泉、白云泉等名泉。

Sprouting Spring • Wanzhu Garden

Built during the Yuan Dynasty (1206-1368) to the west of the Sprouting Spring Park, the over 12000 square meter Wanzhu Garden got its name from the numerous bamboo inside. It is also known as Zhang's Garden for once being the private garden of Zhang Huaizhi (1862-1934), a military governor of Shandong province.

趵突泉·李清照纪念堂

位于趵突泉公园中部漱玉泉旁，1959年，在原丁公（丁宝桢）祠处辟建而成，1999年进行较大规模扩修建。纪念堂采用宋代建筑风格，整个建筑布局精巧和谐，格调朴实、淡雅、大方，恰当地体现了女词人的身份、气质和风度。

Sprouting Spring • Li Qingzhao Memorial Hall

The Memorial was built in 1959 upon the original site of Dinggong Ancestral Temple. It sits next to the Suyu Spring in the middle of the Sprouting Spring Park. The exquisite layout of Song-style buildings match the delicate temperament of Li Qingzhao (1084-1155), the famous ci poet of the Song Dynasty (960-1279).

| 大明湖 · 历下亭 |

　　位于历下区大明湖畔,济南名亭之一,因其南临历山(千佛山),故名历下亭,亦称古历亭。历下亭位于大明湖中最大的湖中岛上,岛面积约4160平方米,历下亭是闻名遐迩的海右古亭。

Daming Lake • Lixia Pavilion

The famous ancient pavilion is located on the largest island in Daming Lake. It is called Lixia Pavilion, or Ancient Li Pavilion, and has Lishan Mountain in the south.

> 大明湖·北极阁

　　位于大明湖东岸，又称真武庙或北极庙，是大明湖景区重要古迹之一，始建于元至元十七年（1280年），是济南市区现存最大的道教庙宇。整个建筑由前后两殿和东西配房及钟鼓楼组成。

Daming Lake • Beiji Pavillion

Also known as Zhenwu Temple or Beiji Temple, the Beiji Pavilion was built in 1280 on the north bank of Daming Lake. It is one of the most important historical sites in the Daming Lake area and the largest Taoist temple in Ji'nan city.

【大明湖·汇波楼】

　　位于大明湖东北岸的北水门之上,明洪武四年(1371年)修建城墙时,在北水门上建了一座两层高的城楼,因城内诸泉水汇流入大明湖,再经北水门流出城外,故命名为汇波楼。1982年在原址重建。

Daming Lake • Huibo Tower

The two-storey gate tower on the north water gate of Daming Lake was originally built in 1371 and was rebuilt in 1982. The springs in the city converge into the Daming Lake and run out of the city through the north water gate. This is how the tower got its name.

大明湖·铁公祠

坐落在大明湖北岸西岸,建于清乾隆五十七年(1792年),是为纪念明代兵部尚书、山东参政铁铉而建。祠堂坐北朝南,为朱红大门,边有半壁曲廊,有石碑与佛公祠相隔。

Daming Lake • Tiegong Ancestral Temple

The temple was built in 1792 on the northwest bank of Daming Lake in memory of Tie Xuan (1366-1402). He was Minister of the Board of War and Canzhizhengshi (an official title of feudal China, equivalent to vice prime minister) of Shandong province during the Ming Dynasty.

大明湖·小沧浪亭

位于大明湖畔铁公祠旁,是一处具有江南风格的小园林。亭子始建于清乾隆五十七年(1792年),由小沧浪亭、曲廊、荷池等组成,系效法苏州沧浪亭风格修建,因规模较小,故取名小沧浪。

Daming Lake • Little Canglang

Little Canglang is a small garden in the style of southern China that was built in 1792 next to the Tiegong Ancestral Temple on the northwest bank of Daming Lake. It was modeled after the Canglang Pavilion in Suzhou but smaller, hence the name "Little Canglang."

大明湖·牌坊

位于大明湖正南,是一座五间七踩重昂单檐式的木结构建筑,为大明湖正门。1984年改为混凝土木结构。整个建筑金碧辉煌,宏伟壮观,被视作大明湖的标志。

Daming Lake • Memorial Archway

The main gate of Daming Lake is a magnificent Memorial Archway located in the south of Daming Lake. Originally a wooden building, it was later transferred to concrete and wooden structure in 1984. It is considered a landmark of the Daming Lake.

灵岩寺·辟支塔

　　位于长清区万德镇灵岩寺内，是园内标志性建筑，始建于宋淳化五年（994年）。塔高54米，为八角九层楼阁式砖塔。塔身青砖砌就，整体造型优美，比例适度，做工精湛。

Lingyan Temple • Pizhi Tower

Pizhi Tower is a landmark inside the Lingyan Temple in Wande Township, Changqing District built in 994 A.D. The tower, at 54 meters tall, is a nine-storey pavilion style tower very well proportioned and beautifully shaped by black bricks.

灵岩寺·千佛殿

　　位于灵岩寺摩顶松北,建于唐贞观年间(627～649年),由惠崇和尚创建,后多次重建。该殿为寺内保存最完好、规模最宏大的建筑。殿内有宋代彩色泥塑罗汉40尊。

Lingyan Temple • Qianfo Hall
Built between 627 and 649 in the north of Moding Pine Tree inside Lingyan Temple by Monk Huichong and rebuilt several times since, the Qianfo Hall is the largest and best-preserved building inside the temple. In the hall are enshrined 40 colored arhat clay sculptures from the Song Dynasty (960-1279).

灵岩寺·千佛殿彩塑

位于千佛殿内,千佛殿内四壁台座上有40尊彩色泥塑罗汉,为宋、明之作,技法精湛,神态各异,喜怒哀乐,栩栩如生,被誉为"海内第一名塑"。壁面上原有明制铜、木小佛千尊,今存293尊。

Lingyan Temple • Colored Sculptures in Qianfo Hall

There are 40 colored arhat clay sculptures enshrined on the altars along the four walls of Qianfo Hall. They are praised as the No. 1 Sculptures within the Four Seas. There were once a thousand small Buddhist sculptures made of copper and wood on the four walls but only 293 have survived.

[灵岩寺·大雄宝殿]

位于山门北，始建于宋代，原名献殿，明正德年间（1506～1521年）鲁王捐资塑大佛像三尊，遂改名为大雄宝殿。

Lingyan Temple • Mahavira Hall

Built in the Song Dynasty (960-1279) north of the main gate, Mahavira Hall, originally called Xian Hall, was renamed during the Ming Dynasty (1368-1644).

灵岩寺·墓塔林

　　位于寺辟支塔西侧，是著名的灵岩寺墓塔林，分布着从北魏到清朝灵岩寺历代高僧的墓塔，现存墓塔167座，铭碑81通，这些墓塔均为全石结构，造型各异。灵岩寺墓塔林是国内最大的石塔林。

Lingyan Temple • Tomb Pagoda Forest

West to the Pizhi Tower stands the tomb pagodas of the respected monks in Lingyan Temple from the North Wei Dynasty (386-534) to the Qing Dynasty (1644-1911). It is the largest stone pagoda forest in the countries with 167 pagodas and 81 tombstones still existing.

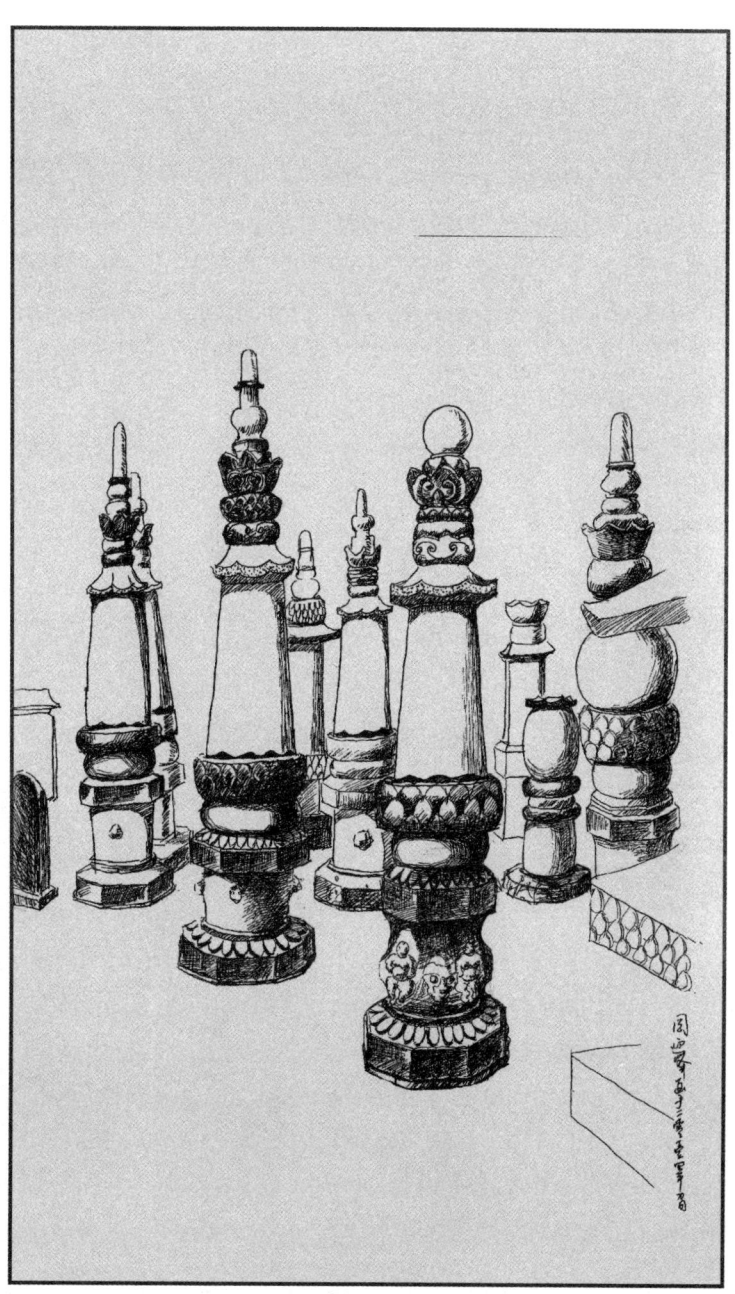

灵岩寺·慧崇塔

位于塔林北端最高处，建于唐天宝年间（742～755年），为灵岩寺高僧慧崇禅师的墓塔。是寺内现存最古老的一座墓塔。该塔为一石砌单层重檐亭阁式塔，高5.3米，宽3.7米，保留有六朝、隋代的艺术风格。

Lingyan Temple • Huichong Tower

Built on the highest ground on the north end of the pagoda forest in 742 to 755, it is the tomb pagoda of Master Huichong, a highly honored monk in the history of Lingyan Temple. At 5.3 meters tall and 3.7 meters wide, Huichong Tower is the oldest pagoda in the temple with the artistic styles of the Six Dynasties (420-581) and Sui Dynasty (581-618).

灵岩寺·天王殿

位于灵岩寺内，建于金末元初。殿中供奉弥勒的化身，即布袋和尚，弥勒菩萨后供奉韦陀菩萨，东西两侧供奉四大天王像。四大天王视察众生的善恶和保护佛法僧三宝。韦陀手持宝杵，是为了镇压魔军，护持佛法。天王殿为山门内第一座重殿，有显正祛邪的意义。

Lingyan Temple • Hall of Heavenly Kings

Built inside the Lingyan Temple near the end of Jin Dynasty (1115-1234) and the beginning of Yuan Dynasty (1206-1368), the Hall of Heavenly Kings is the first grand hall inside the main gate designed to honor the principal of upholding justice and eliminating evil. Inside the hall is enshrined the statute of Maitreya. Behind Maitreya is VEDA Bodhisattva while to the east and west sides there are statues enshrined of the Four Heavenly Kings.

灵岩寺·鼓楼

位于天王殿以北的西侧,建于宋政和四年(1114年)至金皇统元年(1141年)间,由妙空和尚营建,后代不断重修,现为清朝遗物。鼓楼内钟鼓原来都是佛教的法器。凡上堂、小参、普法、入室都要击鼓。

Lingyan Temple • Drum Tower

Built between 1114 and 1141 northwest of the Hall of Heavenly Kings by Master Miaokong, the Drum Tower was rebuilt many times during subsequent dynasties. The current building is from the Qing Dynasty (1644-1911).

灵岩寺·钟楼

在天王殿之北的东侧，北宋末寺内住持妙空所建。钟楼内悬挂的是明正德六年（1511年）住持正昂和尚铸造的铜钟一枚，重量达5000斤。

Lingyan Temple • Bell Tower

The Bell Tower was built by Master Miaokong at the end of the Song Dynasty to the northeast of the Hall of Heavenly Kings. The copper bell that hangs inside the tower was casted by Master Zheng'ang in 1511 and weighs 2500 kilograms.

> 府学文庙

位于历下区明湖路 248 号，北临大明湖，临近芙蓉街等老城街巷。济南府学文庙创建于北宋熙宁年间（1068～1077 年），元末倾塌，明洪武二年（1369 年）重建，清代多次修葺，但基本保持了明朝文庙的规模和建筑布局。

Fuxue Confucian Temple

Located on the south bank of Daming Lake near Furong Street, Fuxue Confucian Temple was initially built during 1068 to 1077 but collapsed near the end of the Yuan Dynasty (1206-1368) and was rebuilt in 1369.

济南清真南大寺

位于市中区永长街南口，原址在历山顶乌满喇巷，元元贞元年（1295年）迁到现在的地址，明弘治七年（1492年）陈玺扩建大殿，南大寺自此始有中国伊斯兰教建筑特色，成为较大规模的古建筑群。

The North Mosque

The North Mosque is an Islamic building with Chinese characteristics relocated to the Libaisi Road at the south end of Yongchang Street. It resided in the Shizhong District from Wumanla Alley on Lishanding Street in 1295. The main hall was expanded in 1492.

济南清真北大寺

位于市中区永长街北首,全国著名清真寺之一,始建于明弘治年间（1488~1505年）,历经沧桑,几经兴衰,是济南西关（回民小区）穆斯林叩拜真主寄托虔诚的圣地,又是学习伊斯兰教义的宗教活动场所。

The South Mosque

As one of the most famous mosques in China, the South Mosque is located inside the Hui community. It was built during the Hongzhi period of the reign of Ming Emperor Zhu Youtang (1488-1505) and is now an important venue for Islamic activities in Xiguan area.

兴福寺

位于槐荫区齐鲁大道与兴福寺路交叉西南，始建于宋代，元代毁于战火，重建于明弘治八年（1495年）。寺院建成后，明万历七年（1579年）、清康熙五十年（1711年）、乾隆二十二年（1757年）都进行过重修。此庙宇有一最大特点是建筑规格较高，大殿和后殿都为庑殿顶的建筑形式，在济南小型庙宇中仅此一处。

Xingfu Temple

Located on the west campus of Ji'nan Vocational College of Nursing, Xifu Temple was built in the Song Dynasty (960-1279). It was destroyed during the Yuan Dynasty (1206-1368) and rebuilt in 1495. The building held a high level of specification. Both the main hall and the back hall have hipped roofs, which is the unique among the small temples in Ji'nan.

长春观

位于市中区长春观街一号,是一座道教全真派宫观。济南民间有"先有长春观,后有济南府"的说法。长春观始建于北宋政和元年(1111年),是济南历史最悠久的道观。元代至清代曾多次重修,现在的长春观建筑为明清所建,后来又经过多次修缮。

Changchun Taoist Temple

Located at No. 1 Changchunguan Street, Ji'nan, the Changchun Taoist Temple is the oldest Taoist temple, dating from 1111, for the Quanzhen branch.

清巡抚院署

位于历下区珍珠泉东侧,建于清康熙五年(1666年),由山东巡抚周有德拆青州明衡王府大殿木料建造。整个建筑金碧辉煌,宏伟壮观。

Shandong Governor's Compound of Qing Dynasty

Built in 1666 to the east of the Pearl Spring by Shandong Governor Zhou Youde, this compound is splendid and magnificent.

31

升阳观

位于历下区寿康楼街四号，该庙供奉八仙之一的吕洞宾，始建于金代，属道教全真龙门派。明末，济南知府樊时英曾重修吕祖庙。清康熙十八年（1679年），在吕祖庙西院修建了一座大殿，名为升阳观。此后，吕祖庙渐渐被人们称为升阳观。

Shengyang Taoist Temple

Originally called Lüzu Temple, Shengyang Taoist Temple was a temple for the Quanzhen Longmen branch of Taoism initially built during the Jin Dynasty (1115-1234). In 1679, a grand hall named Shengyang was built in the west yard of Lüzu Temple. Since then Lüzu Temple gradually became known as Shengyang Taoist Temple.

永济桥

位于平阴县东阿镇浪溪河上，是济南市现存最大跨度的古石拱桥，是山东省艺术价值最高的古石桥之一，原名浪溪桥，根史料记载，建于明弘治十三年（1500年），当时为三孔石桥，后来因为发大水被冲坏。其于明嘉靖三十三年（1554年）改建，更名为永济桥，明隆庆三年（1569年）重修，桥高稍减。

Yongji Bridge

Yongji Bridge, originally named Langxi Bridge, was built in 1500 on the Langxi River in the ancient town of Dong'e. It is an ancient stone arch bridge with the longest span in Ji'nan. It is certainly has one of the highest artistic values of all the stone bridges in Shandong province.

四门塔

位于历城区柳埠镇东北方四千米处，是中国现存唯一的隋代石塔，也是中国现存最早的单层庭阁式石塔。四门塔原属神通寺，该寺始建于前秦皇始元年（351年），是山东境内最早的寺庙，后来庙宇毁于清末大火，剩下四门塔、龙虎塔、九顶塔、墓塔林、摩崖造像等佛教遗址。

Simen Pagoda

Located inside the Shentong Temple 4 km northeast of Liufu Township, Licheng District, Simen Pagoda was built in 351. It is the only existing stone pagoda from the Sui Dynasty (581-618) It is the oldest and most intact single-story stone pagoda in pavilion style in all of China.

九顶塔

始建于唐代，位于南灵鹫山阳九塔寺。因其塔身一塔起，而九顶出而得名。该塔造型华美，国内罕见，日本出版《世界美术全集》称该塔："匠意纵横，构筑奇异，其他无能及"。

Jiuding Tower

Built inside the Jiuta Temple on the South Lingjiu Mountain, Jiuding Tower got its name for its rare appearance. There are nine small towers on the top of the tower, therefore it is called Jiuding (nine roofs) tower.

百脉泉

位于历城区龙泉寺院内,济南五大泉脉之一,与趵突泉齐名。北宋散文家、史学家、政治家曾巩曾云:"岱阴诸泉,皆伏地而发,西则趵突为魁,东则百脉为冠。""百脉寒泉珍珠滚",居章丘八景之首,是中国北方独具特色的泉景公园。

Baimai Spring

Located inside the Longquan Temple, Baimai Spring is one of the top five springs in Ji'nan equally as famous as the Sprouting Spring. It is the first of the eight most popular tourist attractions in Zhangqiu and is quite a unique spring park in northern China.

> 黑虎泉

　　位于历下区环城公园南隅，为天下第一泉风景区的三大泉群之一。通过三个石雕虎头泉水喷出，波澜汹汹，水声喧喧。泉群附近假山平台，回廊曲径，夏日绿树荫荫，鸟语蝉鸣，是游人品茶、玩景之胜地。

Heihu Spring (Black Tiger Spring)

Located on the south bank of the city moat in the southern end of the encircling city park, Heihu Spring is one of the three spring clusters in the No.1 Spring contained within the Four Seas tourist attraction. The adjacent area is a good spot for sipping tea and appreciating the excellent view.

> 珍珠泉

位于历下区大明湖南侧泉城路院前街，今山东省人大常委会大院内西南边。泉池呈长方形，面积为1200多平方米。因为池中遍布着泉眼，不时涌出串串水泡，阳光映照下如同珠玑，故称为珍珠泉，又名"北珍珠泉"。

Pearl Spring

Located on Yuanqian Street, Quancheng Road south of Daming Lake, the square Pearl Spring pool covers an area of 1200 square meters. Strings of bubbles gush from the spring from time to time, looking like pearls in the sun. This is how the spring got its name. It is also referred to as the North Pearl Spring.

五龙潭

　　五龙潭也叫乌龙潭、龙居泉，位于历下区，天下第一泉景区五龙潭公园中部，是三大泉群的主要泉眼之一。据记载，北魏以前称净池，是大明湖的一隅。五龙潭公园内，散布着形态各异的26处古名泉，构成济南四大泉群的五龙潭泉群。

Wulong Pool (Five-Dragon Pool)

Also called Black Dragon Pool or Longju Spring, Wulong Pool is located in the middle of Wulong Pool Park. It is one of the main springs of the top three spring clusters. Inside the park are scattered 26 ancient springs in different shapes.

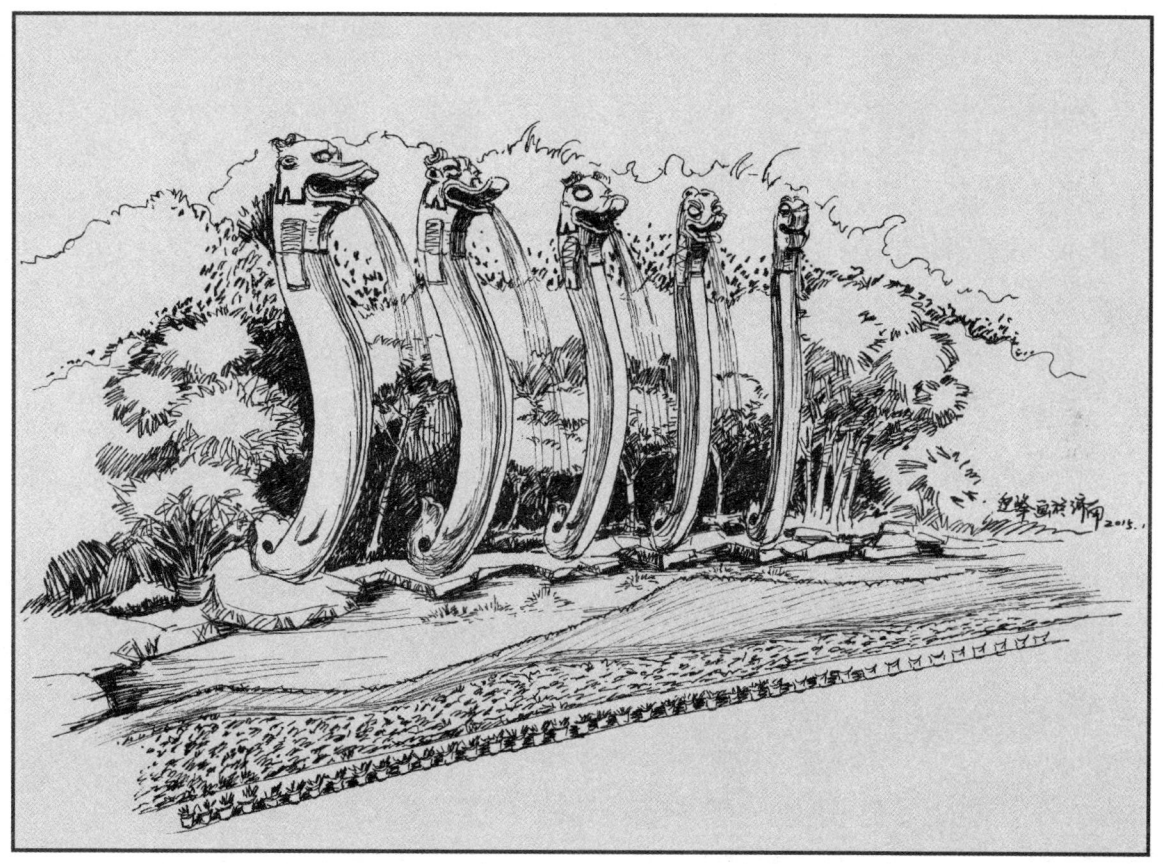

> 千佛山

　　位于济南市区南部，因山上有数不清的佛，所以叫千佛山，海拔285米，面积160多公顷，与趵突泉、大明湖并称济南三大景观，是享誉中外的济南三大名胜之一。

Mount Qianfo

Located in the south of Ji'nan city, Mount Qianfo got its name from the numerous Buddha sculptures in the mountain. (In Chinese, Qianfo means a thousand Buddha.) It is 285 meters high and covers an area of 160 hectares. Mount Qianfo, the Sprouting Spring and the Daming Lake are the top three tourist attractions in Ji'nan.

红叶谷

位于历城区锦绣川水库南 3000 米处，植被覆盖率高达 97%，负氧离子含量是市区的 300 多倍，是"天然氧吧"，故称红叶谷是"泉的源头、云的故乡、花的世界、林的海洋、休闲度假的天堂"。

Hongye Valley
Located three kilometers south of Jinxiuchuan Reservoir. The forest coverage in the area is 97% rich in negative oxygen ions making it a natural oxygen bar.

九如山

位于历城区西营镇,景区面积36平方千米,打造成以"八潭、九瀑、二十四泉、三十六峰"为核心景观,形成了山、瀑、栈、溪、泉为特色的国家级森林公园。

Jiuru Mountain

Located in Xiying Township, Licheng District, Jiuru Mountain covers an area of 36 square kilometers. On the mountain is scattered eight pools, nine waterfalls, 24 springs and 36 peaks making it a beautiful forest park in northern China.

> 曲水亭街

　　位于大明湖南门南侧，是一条闻名中外的历史文化特色老街。曲水亭街连接大明湖、百花洲、王府池子、芙蓉街，文化气息十分浓厚。从珍珠泉和王府池子而来的泉水汇成河，与曲水亭街相依，一边是青砖翠瓦的老屋，一边是绿藻飘摇的清泉。

Qushuiting Street

Located in the south of the south gate of Daming Lake Park, Qushuiting Street is a well-known street with rich historic and cultural deposits. It connects Daming Lake, Baihuazhou Island, Wangfu Pool, and Furong Street.

上新街

　　位于市中区，北起泺源大街，南接文化西路，南高北低，落差有数米，自北而南行走，有步步高升之意，故称"上新街"。20世纪20年代形成街道。这里现存一批近代优秀历史建筑与近代特色民居院落。

Shangxin Street

Connecting Luoyuan Street in the north and West Wenhua Road in the south, Shangxin Street gathers some good historic buildings and unique folk houses. The south end of the street is several meters higher than the north end. Walking up the street from the north to the south means you are moving up step by step, which is why the street is called "Shang Xin Street." (In Chinese, "Shang" means "up" and "Xin" means "new".)

芙蓉街

位于历下区，南临济南泉城路。芙蓉街以街中芙蓉泉而得名。街位于珍珠泉群之中，邻近历代两大府衙和贡院、府文庙及古城主干道。金、明、清时，是文人墨客饮酒赋诗之地。清代诗人董芸曾寓居"芙蓉馆"，因而书声琅琅，流水潺潺，垂柳依依，意境优雅而享誉四海。

Furong Street

Located in downtown Ji'nan in the north of Quancheng Road, Furong Street got its name from the Furong Spring on the street. Around the street scatters the Pearl Spring cluster and not far away are the two state offices with the examination hall of the feudal China, the Confucian Temple and the main street of the old town. In the Jin, Ming and Qing dynasties, men of letters gathered here, writing poems over tea and wine.

> 所里街

位于历下区，司里街小区南区路南，东起太平街，西到双清街，是一条东西长 510 米，宽三米，青石板路面的街道。明崇祯十三年（1640 年）《历城县志》载此街为"所街"。清乾隆年间（1736～1795 年），改为"所里街"。所里街影壁是济南民居中经典的半附墙半独立式的影壁。图中正是该街上的原始影壁，正脊简洁大方，别具一格。

Suoli Street

Located south of the southern part of Silijie Community, Suoli street is three meters wide and 510 meters long. A Quartzite street connecting Taiping Street in the east and Shuangqing Street in the west. The screen wall is half independent, which is classical in the folk houses in Ji'nan. In the picture is the original screen wall on the street with simple and graceful ridges.

章丘朱家峪·文昌阁

原名危阁连云,位于朱家峪村内,山阴朱霞所设计、建造,建于清道光十八年(1838年),距今已有170多年的历史。上建阁楼,下筑阁洞,造型古雅、宏伟而壮观。楼洞一体,全用大型青方石筑成,历尽沧桑,坚不可摧。

Zhangqiu Zhujiayu Village • Wenchang Pavilion

Located in Zhujiayu village, Wenchang Pavilion (originally called Wei Ge Lian Yun) was designed and built by Zhu Xia over 170 years ago in 1838 with large bluestones. It remains intact.

章丘朱家峪·祠堂

位于章丘市朱家峪村，明洪武年间（1368～1398年），朱氏家族迁到该村。村内祠堂，创建于清光绪八年（1882年），体现了朱氏家族重视文化的传统。现存建筑建于1937年，推拉式铁质祠门别具一格，美观大方。

Zhangqiu Zhujiayu Village • The Zhu's Ancestral Memorial

Located in Zhujiayu Village, Guanzhuang Township, Zhangqiu City, the Memorial was built in 1882 and renovated 60 years later in 1932. The Memorial showed the Zhu's family values on traditional culture. The iron push-pull gate is quite unique.

章丘朱家峪·康熙立交桥

位于朱家峪村内，建造于清康熙九年（1670年），至今300余年。立交古桥分东西两座，相距约十余米，上下行人，通车运输，十分方便。桥身全用小型青石叠砌而成，历尽风雨雪霜，未曾损坏，依然保持原貌，被专家誉为"现代立交桥的雏形"。

Zhangqiu Zhujiayu Village • Kangxi Overpasses

Located in Zhujiayu village, the overpasses were built over 300 years ago in 1670 during the reign of Qing Emperor Kangxi. The two overpasses are several meters apart in the east and west and are made from small bluestones. They remain intact after all these years.

近代建筑
Modern Architecture

将军庙天主教堂

位于历下区将军庙街西首路北。教堂奉无染原罪圣母为主保,全名为圣母无染原罪堂,百姓称之为将军庙街天主堂,可追溯到16世纪,由主教堂、小修道院、主教公署组成。该建筑融合中外,兼采南北,特别是内部壁画精美,是济南重要的宗教建筑之一。

Jiangjunmiao Catholic Church

Built on the north side of Jiangjunmiao Street in the 16th century, the Church consists of the main church, priory, and the bishop's house. It is an important venue for religious activities.

洪家楼天主教堂

位于历城区洪楼广场北侧，是华北地区规模最大的天主教堂，始建于清光绪二十七年（1901年），清光绪三十一年（1905年）建成。教堂为双塔哥特式建筑，是中国三大著名天主教堂之一，也是济南文化带的重要象征。

Hongjialou Catholic Church

Built on the north side of Honglou Square in Licheng District from 1901 to 1905, the Church is a double-towered gothic building. It is the largest Catholic church in northern China and one of the three most famous Catholic churches in all of China.

林家庄天主教堂

位于历城区林家庄，北临经十东路，南临林家庄小区。清光绪三十二年（1906年），由德国传教士筹建，工程耗时约两年。2003年扩建新堂，新建教堂坐南朝北。

Linjiazhuang Catholic Church

Located between East Jingshi Road in the north and Linjiazhuang Residence Community in the south, the church was built in 1906 by German missionaries. The construction took approximately two years. On October 28, 2003 a founding ceremony for the new north-facing church was held.

陈家楼天主教堂

位于天桥区前陈家楼63号，建于清宣统元年（1909年），时命名为"大圣若瑟堂"。其建筑为砖石结构，是一座哥特式的天主教堂，分设礼拜堂、钟楼、膳宿室等房舍。

Chenjialou Catholic Church

Located at No. 63 Qianchenjialou Street in Tianqiao District, Chenjialou Catholic Church was named St. Joseph's Church when built in 1909. The church building is in the gothic style with brick-and-stone structure, covering an area of 667 square meters.

[英国浸礼会礼拜堂]

　　位于齐鲁医院内，教堂建于清光绪三十一年（1905年），是齐鲁大学神学院的配套工程，由外国牧师设计，有晚期哥特式教堂的特点，现为山东大学齐鲁医院的职工食堂。

British Baptist Church

Located inside the Qilu Hospital, the church was built in 1905 as a supporting facility for the divinity school of Qilu University. The church was designed by a foreign missionary and features late gothic style architecture.

后宰门街基督教礼拜堂

也称百花洲基督教堂，因位于历下区后宰门街，又称后宰门教堂，为济南现有的七处基督教教堂之一，位于历下区后宰门街西首路北，西临曲水亭街，北临百花洲南岸，在曲水垂柳的掩映下，显得分外幽静。

Houzaimen Christian Church

Located on the west end of Houzaimen Street on the north side with Qushuiting Street to the west and Baihuazhou Lake to the north, Houzaimen Christian Church, also known as Baihuazhou Christian Church, is one of the seven existing Christian churches in Ji'nan.

> 济南德国领事馆

　　位于市中区经二纬二路口西北角，今济南市人民政府院内。该建筑为济南商埠地区的早期西式建筑之一，对火车站一带德国建筑风格的形成具有重要影响。

Original Site of German Consulate to Ji'nan

Located on the northwest corner of Jing'er and Wei'er crossroad inside the current yard of the Ji'nan Municipal Government, the building is one of the earliest western-style buildings in the Ji'nan business area and has a great influence in the German-style architecture in the area around the railway station.

济南日本总领事馆

　　位于市中区经三路 240 号，由总领事馆邸、办公楼、办事人员宿舍、厩舍和庭园组成，造型体现为日本仿西洋古典形式风格，受日耳曼式建筑的影响。第二次世界大战爆发后，日本在侵华战争中再次占领济南，1938 年重建，并突击设计施工，于 1939 年 8 月在原址落成。

Original Site of Japanese Consulate to Ji'nan

Located at No. 240 Jingsan Road, the building complex includes the Consulate, office building, dorm, barn and the yard. The buildings are in a classic western style with heavy German influence.

济南美国领事馆

1918年10月美国驻济南领事馆正式成立,经历了多次开馆、闭馆。领事馆最初位于经五路纬二路东,1916年起迁往经二路纬二路西南角。1921年起又迁至经七路、小纬二路东北角。

Original Site of American Consulate to Ji'nan

Located inside the International Cultural Exchange Center of Shandong Province, the former American Consulate to Ji'nan was officially set up in October 1918. After years of ups and downs, the consulate was relocated from the east side of Wei'er and Jingwu crossroad to the southwest corner of Jing'er and Wei'er crossroad in 1916. It was later moved to the northeast corner of Jingqi and Little Wei'er crossroad in 1921.

济南老火车站

是19世纪末20世纪初德国著名建筑师赫尔曼·菲舍尔设计的一座典型的德式车站建筑。它曾是亚洲最大的火车站,世界上唯一的哥特式建筑群落,登上清华、同济的建筑类教科书,并曾被战后西德出版的《远东旅行》列为远东第一站。

Old Ji'nan Railway Station

Located on the site of the current Ji'nan Railway Station, the old railway station building was designed by famous German architect Hans Fischer in late 19th century and early 20th century. The classic German railway building was once the largest railway station in Asia and, at that time, the only gothic architectural complex in the world.

> 黄台车站

　　位于历下区胶济铁路约 378 千米处，初始称为东关车站，也称为济南东站，自清光绪三十年（1904 年）建站至今，已有 110 年历史。黄台车站站舍是典型的欧式建筑，与车站东南的洪家楼教堂建筑群遥相辉映。

Huangtai Railway Station

Located at about 378 km on Jiaoji railway, Huangtai railway station it was originally known as Dongguan Station or Ji'nan East Station. The station was built in 1904 and has a history of over 100 years. It is a classic European-style building echoing the Hongjialou Church on its the southeast side.

津浦铁路洛口黄河大桥

　　位于济南市北部，是津浦铁路上的一座跨河大桥。北岸是鹊山东麓，南岸是洛口古渡口。大桥由德国孟阿斯桥梁公司承建，清光绪三十四年（1908年）开工，1921年竣工通车。

Tiensin-Pukow Railway Luokou Bridge over the Yellow River

To the north of Ji'nan, this is a railway bridge on the Tiensin-Pukow railway linking the east side of Queshan Mountain in the north and Luokou Ancient Port in the south. The bridge was built by a German bridge company in 1908 and was opened to traffic in 1921.

济南府电报收发局

位于天桥区经一路91号，建于清光绪三十年（1904年），为济南现存最早的电讯建筑，采用巴洛克建筑风格。1929年后改作车站邮局，部分用于开设招待所，现由济南市邮政局管理使用。

Ji'nan Municipal Telegraph Bureau

Built in 1904 at No. 91, Jingyi Road, Tianqiao District, the Baroque-style building is the earliest telegraph building still standing today in Ji'nan.

| 瑞蚨祥布店 |

位于市中区经二路 215 号,建于 1923 年,是瑞蚨祥在济南商迹的最后一处建筑,如今还在营业。该店铺的建筑布局,坐北朝南,采用传统的四合院形式,店铺正立面则体现了中西合璧的风格。该建筑是山东省优秀历史建筑,也是济南民族工业的发祥地。

Ruifuxiang Cloth Store

Built in 1923 at No. 215, Jing'er Road, Shizhong District, it is the last building left of Ruifuxiang's operation in Ji'nan. The south-facing store is in the form of the traditional quadrangle courtyard and is still in business today.

| 英美烟草公司 |

　　位于市中区经四路小纬二路交口东北角，为假三层文艺复兴风格建筑，建成于1919年，建筑平面呈"凹"型，中部入口处外凸，高台阶步入门厅，门厅外立古典柱式，上方的阳台按照石柱的布局分出层次。

British American Tobacco China

Built in 1919 on the northeast corner of Jingsi and Little Wei'er crossroad, This is a false-three-story building in the renaissance style.

> 丰大洋行

　　旧址位于济南市纬六路 27 号，始建于 1919 年，总建筑面积 600 平方米，是济南商埠区保存较完整、具有巴洛克建筑风格的孤本。

Fengda Foreign Bank

Located at No. 27 Wei'liu Road, the former Shandong Fengda Bank was built in 1919 and covered an area of 600 square meters. It is the only well-preserved Baroque-style building in Ji'nan's old business area.

[德华银行济南分行旧址]

位于市中区经二纬一路西口，德式建筑，建于清光绪二十七年（1901年），最初为黄河铁路大桥德国工程师的住宅，清光绪三十二年（1906年）年改为德华银行，它是济南的第一家外商银行。该建筑主体二层，局部三层，主屋面顶部的小望楼和八角形塔楼均为双层变折式屋顶，错落有致。

Former Site of the Ji'nan Branch of Deutsche Asiatische Bank
Built in 1901 on the northeast corner of at the crossroad of Jing'er Road and Wei'er Road, the building was originally the residence of the German engineers for the railway bridge project on the Yellow River. It was made to house the Deutsche Asiatische Bank that was the first foreign bank in Ji'nan.

济南交通银行大厦

位于德华银行济南分行东侧。该建筑建于1925年，设计者为中国建筑师庄俊，风格基本上为早期仿希腊古典复兴式。

Ji'nan Bank of Communications

Built in 1925 on the east side of the Ji'nan Branch of Deutsche Asiatische Bank, the building was designed by Chinese architect Zhuang Jun. It was modeled on the early Greek period classical revival architecture.

山东大学堂

即山东大学前身,是继京师大学堂之后中国创办的第二所官立大学堂。清光绪二十七年(1901年),山东巡抚袁世凯上奏《山东试办大学堂暂行章程折稿》,同时调蓬莱知县李于锴进行筹备,是年11月《折稿》获准,在济南泺源书院正式创办了官立山东大学堂,周学熙任管理总办(校长)。

Shandong Imperial University

Shandong Imperial University, the predecessor of Shandong University, was the second government-funded university in China after the Imperial University of Peking. Its founding was granted in 1901 after the then Shandong governor Yuan Shikai submitted a proposal to the throne and Zhou Xuexi was appointed as the president of the university.

齐鲁大学·办公楼

位于山东大学西校区,原名齐鲁大学办公楼,始建于1923年,是校园中最早的建筑之一。建筑北立面三层,南立面四层,屋顶歇山交叉,高高翘起的翼角极富中国传统韵味,是中国建筑复兴样式的代表。

Cheeloo University • Office Building

Built in 1923 on the west campus of Shandong University, the office building of Cheeloo University is one of the earliest buildings on campus.

齐鲁大学・考文楼

　　位于山东大学西校区，是一座较典型的中西合璧式建筑，是齐鲁大学建校初期建造的主要教学建筑之一，为纪念齐鲁大学的创始人之一狄考文而命名的。建筑坐南面北，主体三层，东西两端为单层。建筑的平面、立面运用西洋古典主义手法，分为三段处理。

Cheeloo University • Mateer Hall

Located on the west campus of Shandong University, Mateer Hall is a classic building combining the features of both Chinese and Western architecture. It was one of the main buildings in the early days of Cheeloo University and was named after Di Kaowen(Calvin Wilson Mateer), one of the founders of Cheeloo University.

齐鲁大学·柏根楼

位于山东大学西校区，是原齐鲁大学一幢典型的中西合璧式建筑，也是齐鲁大学建校初期的主要教学建筑之一，为纪念齐鲁大学的前身之一——广文大学的首任校长美国柏尔根而命名的。

Cheeloo University • Bergen Hall

Located in the west campus of Shandong University, Bergen Hall is another classic building combining both the features of Chinese and Western architecture. It is also one of the main buildings in the early days of Cheeloo University. It was named after Paul D. Bergen, the first president of Guangwen University(Shantung Christian University), the predecessor of Cheeloo University.

齐鲁大学医学院·共合楼

位于齐鲁医院内,是 1914 年在英国浸礼会资助下兴建的养病楼。为三层砖混结构,建筑平面布局对称,南部是主入口,门前石砌台阶,大门为欧洲古典券柱式,整个建筑平面呈哑铃状。

Cheeloo University Medical School • Gonghe Building

Located inside QiluCceeloo Hospital, this is a health care building constructed in 1914 with the funding from the British Baptist church. The three-storey concrete-brick building has a symmetrical structure with the middle part protruding. The main entrance is in the south part with stone stairs at the front and a classic arch-column gate.

齐鲁大学医学院·求真楼

位于齐鲁医院共合楼东面，建于清宣统三年（1911年），是一座坐南朝北的砖石建筑。平面结构分三部分，中间主体部分前后方向突出，两层，兼有地下室。东西两翼进深缩小，为单层坡面平房。整个建筑中西合璧，和谐统一。

Cheeloo University Medical School • Qiuzhen Building

Located in the east of Gonghe Building, Qiuzhen Building was a south facing brick and stone building constructed in 1911. The plane structure consists of three parts. The two-storey main body in the middle protrudes in both front and back; while the east and west wings are single-storey bungalows with reduced depth.

齐鲁大学医学院·新兴楼

位于齐鲁医院内,建于清宣统三年(1911年),原为医学大讲堂,今为办公二楼。

Cheeloo University Medical School • Xinxing Building

Located inside Qilu(Cheeloo) Hospital, Xinxing Building, and constructed in 1911, it was originally the medical lecture hall and is the currently the No.2 office building.

济南懿范女子中学

位于山东大学老校区内，始建于1936年，由美国的天主教玛利亚修女会所创办。建筑均采用灰砖，坡屋顶上覆以红瓦，该校园与周边的洪家楼天主教堂等构成了济南的一处较大的天主教教会建筑群，典型的欧洲建筑风格。

Ji'nan Yifan Middle School for Girls

Located on the old campus of Shandong University, the Ji'nan Yifan Middle School for Girls was built in 1936 by Sisters of Mercy from the United States. The buildings are in classic European style with grey bricks and red tiles on sloping roofs.

广智院

位于广智院街,清光绪三十年(1904年),英国传教士怀恩光在青州建立了一所"博古堂",后迁到济南,改名为"广智院",是济南乃至我国最早的博物院之一。建设之初,广智院设计了"回"字形的陈列室、阅览室、研究所、布道堂。

Guangzhiyuan Museum

Located in Guangzhiyuan Street, the Museum is one of the earliest museums in Ji'nan as well as all of China. In 1904, British missionary John Sutherland Whitewright founded an Antique Hall in Qingzhou, which was later relocated to Ji'nan and renamed Guangzhi Museum.

同仁会济南医院

位于省立医院内，建于 20 世纪 30 年代，整体建筑为日本明治维新后兴起的带有和风的老摩登风格，在济南的老城与商埠区都为难得的大型医疗建筑，现为山东省立医院。

Tongrenhui Ji'nan Hospital Main Building

Located in the provincial hospital, the building was built in the 1930s in the old modern architectural style with Japanese features that were popular after the Meiji restoration. It is a large hospital building rarely seen in the old downtown and business area of Ji'nan.

| 山东红卍字会施诊所 |

　　位于魏家庄大街和麟祥街之间，1928年建成，1942年称红卍字会附属医院，1953年停办。建筑是依中轴线展开的，由前后中三进院落组成的四合楼群。

The Red Swastika Society Clinic of Shandong Province

Located between Weijiangzhuang Street and Linxiang Street, the clinic was built in 1928 and named the Red Swastika Society Affiliated Hospital in 1942 but ceased operation in 1953. The buildings spread along the central axis and form a quadrangle building complex with three courtyards in the front, middle and back.

解放阁

位于历下区下河涯街 22 号，近黑虎泉西路。1963 年，利用原内城东南城角砌筑台基，以纪念济南战役的胜利。20 世纪 80 年代初，在台上建阁，1988 年建成，通高 30 米，面积 620 平方米，为二层楼阁式建筑。

Jiefang Pavilion

Located at No. 22 Xiaheya Street near Heihu Spring West Road, a podium was built in 1963 in the southeast corner of the inner city wall in memorial to the victory of Ji'nan Battle. In the early 1980s, a two-storey pavilion 30 meters high was built on the podium in memory of the martyrs that died during the liberation war.

> 跳伞塔

位于历下区经十路全民健身中心内，建于 1956 年的跳伞塔，高 61 米，曾是济南市最高建筑。随着以跳伞塔为中心的原济南市体校地块建成我市最大的全民健身中心，跳伞塔也再次迎来辉煌。

Skydiving Tower

Built in 1956, the Skydiving Tower is located inside the Public Fitness Center and was once the tallest building in Ji'nan. It was listed as the third batch of cultural relic protection sites in 2007.

宏济堂

位于市中区经二纬五路，清光绪二十八年（1902 年），北京同仁堂少东家乐镜宇捐山东候补道来济，依山东巡抚杨士骧在院前大街举办山东官药局，清光绪三十三年（1907 年）取得山东官药局承受权，改名为宏济堂药店。清光绪三十年（1904 年），济南开埠，1920 年 8 月，乐镜宇在商埠兴建宏济堂西号，该建筑中西合璧，是济南商埠建筑的典型代表之一。

Hongjitang Museum
Built in 1902 on Jing'er and Weiwu road by Le Jingyu, the young lord of Beijing Tongrentang Drugstore, the building combines the Chinese and Western architectural styles and is a classic representation of the buildings in Ji'nan's old business area.

山东省实验中学老校门

位于市中区经二纬五路，始建于清光绪三十年（1904年），前身是山东大学堂校门，颇具古典学府风格，1992年由于经七路拓宽拆除重建。

The Old Gate of Shandong Experimental High School

Located at No. 73 Jingqi Street, the original building was the gate of Shandong Imperial University built in 1904. It was rebuilt in 1992.

山东省济南第一中学旧址

位于历下区运署街43号,始建于清光绪二十九年(1903年),有着浓厚的文化氛围和悠久的育人传统。100多年来济南一中培养了一代又一代的社会英才。众多近代著名学者、作家曾在这里读书、学习、任教。

The Original Site of Ji'nan No. 1 High School

Built in 1903 at No. 43 Yunshu Street, the school has a long history of rich cultural deposits. Many famous scholars and writers in modern times have studied and taught in the school.

[金氏公馆]

位于市中区共青团路麟趾巷30号，现在为济南市伊斯兰教协会会址。洋楼平面上近于方形，大门开于南边，蹬上六级的半圆形台阶，其上是中间突出的三开间、二层的外柱廊。柱廊每层有四根白色石柱，柱身光洁无凹槽，柱头为爱奥尼克样式。

The Jin's Residence

Located at No. 35, Linzhi Alley, Gongqingtuan Road, the building now houses the Islamic Association of Ji'nan. The building is a square horizontally with the main gate in the south. Up on the six-step half-circle stairs is a two-story colonnade three kaijian wide protruding in the middle. There are two white stone columns with ionic chapiters on each floor. (Translator's note: kaijian is the standard width of a room in an old-style house. 1 kaijian is about 3.3 meters.)

> 老舍旧居

　　又称老舍纪念馆，位于历下区南新街58号，是老舍先生1931～1934年在齐鲁大学任教时的居所。

Laoshe Memorial

Located at No. 58 Nanxin Street, Lixia District, this was the residence of Laoshe (1899-1966), a famous Chinese writer. He lived here from 1931 to 1934 when he was teaching at Cheeloo University.

> 泉城广场

位于历下区泺源大街,是济南市的中心广场,地处山、泉、河、城怀抱之中。广场东西长约780米,南北宽约230米。设计以贯通趵突泉、解放阁的边线为主轴,以榜棚街和泺文路的延续为副轴而构成框架。各功能分区围绕轴线由西向东依次展开。

Spring City Square
Located in the center of Ji'nan, the Spring City Square is 780 meters long from east to west and 230 meters wide from south to north, covering an area of about 1,660,000 square meters.

民俗文化
Folk Arts

山东吕剧

　　吕剧是山东省汉族戏曲剧种之一，曾名化装扬琴、琴戏，由汉族民间说唱艺术山东琴书发展演变而来，起源于山东以北黄河三角洲，流行于山东和江苏、安徽部分地区。1953年，山东省吕剧院成立之后，吕剧成为遍及山东、享誉全国的剧种。

Shangdong Lü Opera

Lü Opera, once known as Yang-chin in Makeup or Qin Opera, is one of the operas of the Han nationality. It evolved from the Shandong Qinshu, story-telling folk art, that is told mainly in song, with musical accompaniment. It originated from the Yellow River Delta north of Shandong, and has been popular in Shandong, Jiangsu, and part of Anhui province.

山东皮影

　　济南皮影戏又称兰州布影、滦州布影，是一门古老的汉族传统艺术。由于口误，叫成兰州布影。"兰"实为"滦"字之误。1952年，改称为山东皮影。西方戏剧史家曾说过："中国的皮影是电影的开山祖。"

Shandong Leather Silhouettes Show

Also known as Lanzhou Cloth Shadow show or Luanzhou Cloth Shasow show, Shandong Leather Silhouettes Show is an ancient art form of the Han nationality popular in such area as Zaozhuang, Linyi, Ji'ning, Qingdao and Yantai. The player controls the Silhouettes from behind the curtain to the accompaniment of an instrument.

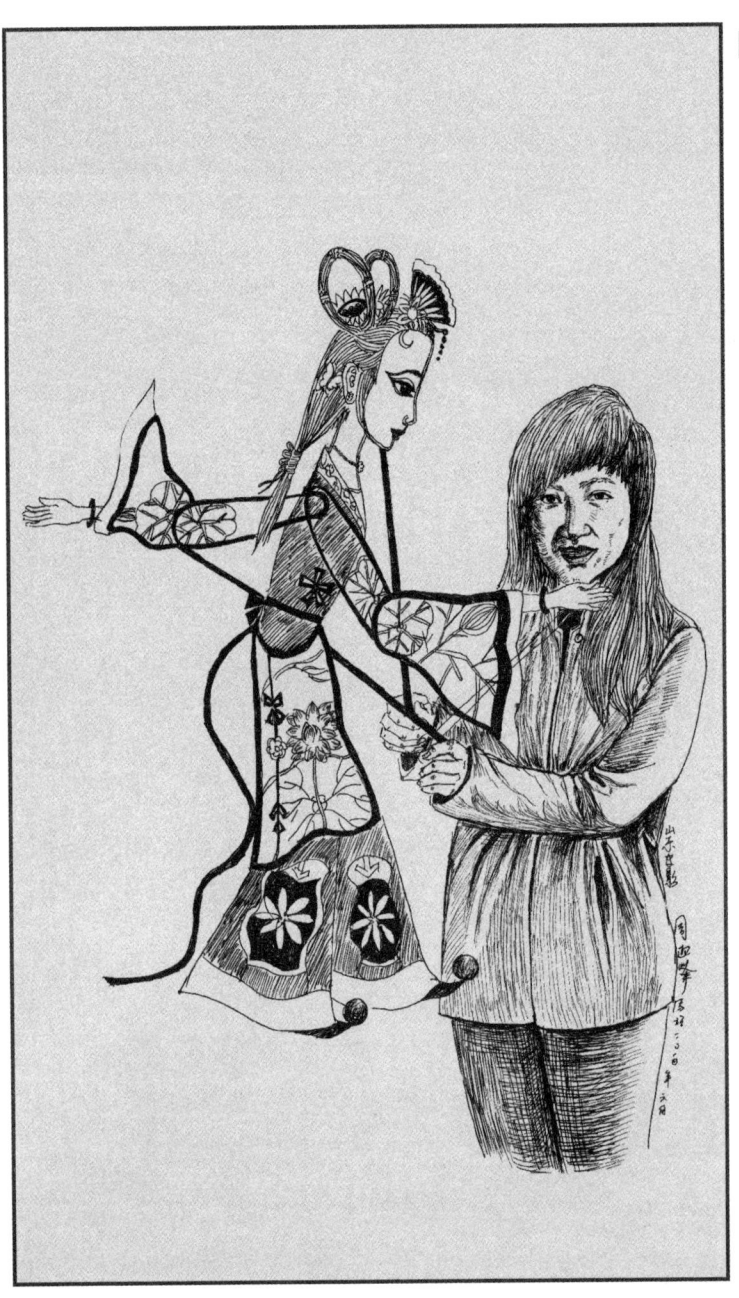

山东琴书

　　山东琴书是山东地区汉族曲艺品种之一,又称小曲子、唱扬琴、山东洋琴等,发源于鲁西南的菏泽地区,产生于清代乾隆年间(1736～1795年),原为农民自娱的庄家耍(又叫玩局)。清末呈现兴盛局面,名家辈出,流传地区日益广泛。

Shandong Qinshu

Shandong Qinshu, also called Small Songs, Singing Yang-chin, or Shandong Yang-chin, is one of the many folk art forms of the Han nationality in Shandong. It originated from the Heze area in southwest Shandong in the early days during the reign of Qing Emperor, Qianlong (1736-1795). Usually there are two to five artists on stage during a performance.

> 山东大鼓

　　是北方大鼓之鼻祖,形成于明代末期,已有近 400 年的历史,主要流传于以山东省菏泽为中心的广大鲁、苏、豫地区。其原称犁铧大鼓,因其伴奏乐器为犁铧碎片而得名,自《老残游记》之后,始谐音美其称为"梨花大鼓"。

Shandong Drum

As the originator of the drum art in northern China, Shandong Drum had taken form over 350 years ago at the end of the Ming dynasty (1368-1644). It has been popular in the area around Heze city including Shandong, Jiangsu and He'nan provinces. It was formerly called Lihua (Ploughshare) Drum because the accompaniment instrument included fragments of ploughshare.

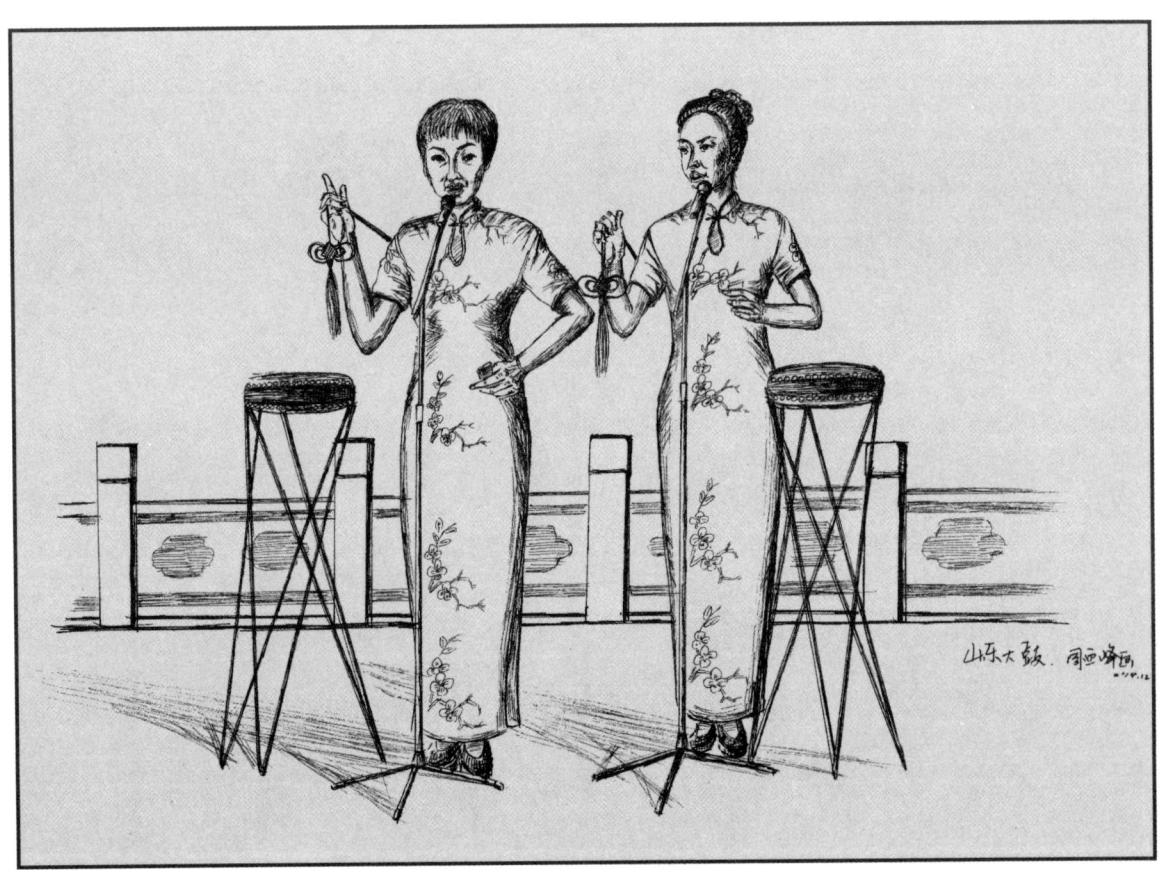

山东快书

是起源于山东省的汉族传统曲艺形式，发源于山东省临清、济宁、兖州一带，具有100多年的历史。它最早流行于山东、华北、东北各地，新中国成立后发展遍及全国。演唱者手执竹板或鸳鸯板，以快节奏击板叙唱，故又名竹板快书。

Shandong Clapper Ballad

Shandong Clapper Ballad is a traditional folk art of the Han nationality originated from Shandong province over 100 years ago. It spread from Shandong in the north and northeast of China to the whole country after the founding of PRC. The performers hold a pair of bamboo clappers or yuanyang (Chinese duck) clappers, and sing a storytelling ballad to the fast beat of clappers. As a result, it is also called bamboo clapper ballad.

山东木板大鼓

是济南市历城地区的一种汉族曲艺形式。木板大鼓行腔变化无穷，喜处高亢豪放，悲处委婉苍凉。其表演风格幽默风趣，演员要有较深的戏剧表演基础，通过形体模仿和语言化妆，达到形似、神似，引领听众进入曲中。

Shandong Wood Plate Drum

A folk art form of the Han nationality in Licheng district of Ji'nan, the Wood Plate Drum features free-style narration and ballad in long or short verses. The stage, lighting, instrument or props do not restrict the venue for performance.

> 五音戏

是山东地区的独有汉族戏曲剧种，有 200 多年的历史，起源于山东省的章丘、历城一带，传于济南、淄博、滨州、潍坊等地。其原名肘鼓子（或周姑子）戏，以唱腔优美动听，语言生动风趣，表演朴实细腻而著称，地方特色浓郁。

Five-tone Drama

Formerly known as Zhouguzi Drama, it is a type of drama exclusive to the Han nationality in Shandong province. It originates from Zhangqiu and Licheng area and has been popular in such areas as Ji'nan, Zibo, Binzhou and Weifang with a history of over 200 years. The Drama featured beautiful melodies and witty lyrics with many specific local characteristics.

平阴木偶戏

是山东省的汉族传统戏剧，属于北方杖头木偶，清雍正十年（1732年）由郜钦从外地传入，并组建木偶戏班距，今已有280余年的历史，主要流行于安城乡、旧县乡、洪范池镇等山区。

Pingyin Puppet Show

Pingyin Puppet Show, a traditional opera of the Han nationality in Shandong province is over 270 years old and has been popular in such mountainous areas as Ancheng, Jiuxian and Hongfanchi townships.

> 柳子戏

又称弦子戏，黄河以北有糠窝窝、百调子、吹腔之称呼，是中国汉族戏曲古老声腔之一。中国戏曲史上曾有"东柳、西梆、南昆、北弋"之称的"东柳"就是山东柳子戏。

Liuzi Opera

Also known as Xianzi Opera, Liuzi Opera is an ancient tune of Chinese operas of the Han nationality. In the history of Chinese opera, there are four prominent schools, namely, Liu in the East, Bang in the West, Kun in the south and Yi in the north. The Liu in the East refers to the Liuzi Opera in Shandong province.

商河鼓子秧歌

　　鼓子秧歌是山东省的汉族民间舞蹈，最初起源于济南商河县，有1000多年的历史，是汉族民间为庆丰收而载歌载舞的一种艺术形式。

Shanghe Drum Yangko Dance

Originated from Shanghe County of Ji'nan over 1000 years ago, Drum Yangko Dance is a folk dance celebrating the harvest. It is quite popular in the Han nationality.

> 济南相声

济南相声是山东省济南市的汉族传统曲艺，济南市级非物质文化遗产，于20世纪20年代由北京传入，40年代开始盛行，以茶社收费的形式向观众表演。2006年，济南最负盛名的晨光相声大会又重新开始延续过去的辉煌，开始免费相声演出。

Ji'nan Cross-talk

Cross-talk was born in Beijing and spread to Ji'nan in the 1920s and became popular in the 1940s. It is most often performed in teahouses.

高跷"乔家"

曲堤镇乔家上杠高跷是非物质文化遗产保护项目,技术高、花样多、惊险刺激,惹人喜爱,具有鲜明的地方特色,其套路丰富多彩、动作灵活多变,尤其是上杠、跳人、上木板、打劈叉等高难度动作,更是惊险刺激,扣人心弦,具有很高的艺术欣赏价值。

The Qiao's Stilts Dance

As one of the intangible cultural heritages, the Qiao's Stilts Dance in Qudi Township has distinctive local features. It features a great variety of breath-taking skills of high artistic value, which makes it very popular.

章丘龙舞

章丘的舞龙始于明朝，境内舞龙的村庄很多，其中，文祖镇西王黑村的龙灯最有名气。随着民间扮玩的发展，龙灯陆续遍布章丘境内。清末，章丘的一些民间艺人到外地做生意，把舞布龙的技艺学了回来。之后，境内便形成了夜间扮玩舞龙灯，白天扮玩舞布龙的定式。

Zhangqiu Dragon Dance

Zhangqiu Dragon Dance started in the late Ming dynasty (1368-1644) and early Qing dynasty (1644-1911). Some folk artists learned the trick of dragon dance when they were doing business out of town. Gradually, a tradition had taken place in Zhangqiu to play dragon lantern at night and perform dragon dance during the day. The dragon dance combines instrument playing with dance.

阿胶制作工艺

阿胶始于秦汉，至今已有2000多年的历史了，为传统的滋补、补血上品，是以驴皮为主要原料，放阿井之水而制成（不放阿井水熬煮的胶为驴皮胶、驴胶）。阿胶原产山东省古东阿县，佳者带琥珀色，透明，无臭味。其传统熬胶技艺也已被列入国家级非物质文化遗产名录。

Donkey-hide Gelatin Craftsmanship

The production of donkey-hide gelatin under "Fu" brand has inherited the essence of the 2500-year gelatin production experiences in Dong'e township. The, Fu brand developed a unique production line and quality monitoring system that combines modern technology with older, traditional techniques.

济南油旋制作工艺

　　油旋是济南传统名吃,外皮酥脆,内瓤柔嫩,葱香透鼻,因其形似螺旋,表面油润呈金黄色,故名油旋。油旋有圆形和椭圆形两种。

Ji'nan Youxuan Making Technic

Youxuan is a traditional food in Ji'nan. It is a round or oval flat pastry made of dough. It is soft in its interior and crispy outside with strong smell of cooked green onion. The pastry got its name for its golden color and spiral-shaped center. (In Chinese, You means cooking oil, Xuan means spiral.)

龙山黑陶制作技艺

龙山黑陶，是继仰韶文化彩陶之后的优秀品种，古老的制陶技艺，是距今4000多年前中国新石器时代晚期的一种文化。它以黑色陶器为其特征，所以称之为黑陶文化，因1928年首次发现于山东省济南市章丘市龙山街道的城子崖，所以又称龙山文化。

Longshan Black Pottery Craftsmanship

Longshan Black Pottery civilization dates back over 4000 years ago into the late New Stone Age in China. The civilization is characterized by black pottery, an ancient pottery making technique. It was discovered in 1928 for the first time in Chengziya, Longshan community of Zhangqiu. Therefore, it is also called Longshan civilization.

商河老粗布制作技艺

商河老粗布传统纺织技艺历史悠久，1000多年前就在商河大地产生，明清民国时期制度达到了繁荣，在商河民间形成了女子14岁纺线，16岁织布的习俗。

Shanghe Handwoven Cloth Craftsmanship

Cloth weaving appeared over 1000 years ago and was quite prosperous during the Ming (1368-1644) and Qing (1644-1911) dynasties as well as the Republic of China (1912-1949). In Shanghe, there was a tradition that girls began to learn doubling thread at the age of 14 and weaving cloth at the age of 16.

玉谦旗袍制作技艺

玉谦旗袍制作工艺始于清同治年间（1862~1874年），玉谦旗袍在山东济南大名鼎鼎，店门前的那副对联"门前圣水芙蓉泉，旗袍世家数百年"可见一斑。

Yuqian Cheongsam Craftsmanship

Yuqian Cheongsam is well known in Ji'nan since the reign of Qing Emperor Tongzhi (1862-1874). From the 1930s to the 1990s, Yu Chengzhan, the fourth generation inheritor of Yuqian Cheongsam Store, was a well-known figure in the Spring City for his Cheongsam craftsmanship.

崮山馍馍制作技艺

相传乾隆皇帝南巡时,耳闻崮山馍馍名气,品尝后,龙颜大悦,为崮山馍馍点上了象征"福禄喜寿"的梅花标记。历经400多年岁月,曾经的贡品——崮山馍馍已走进寻常百姓家。

Gushan Steamed Bun Craftsmanship

Legend says than when Qing Emperor Qianlong (1736-1795) heard about the reputation of the Gushan Steamed Bun on his tour in South China, he asked for it and was very happy after tasting it. So he put a plum blossom sign on the bun symbolizing happiness and blessing. Over 400 years later, the bun for tribute has now become a household food.

鲁绣

鲁绣一种古老的汉族传统刺绣工艺，山东地区的代表性刺绣，也是历史文献中记载最早的一个绣种，属中国八大名绣之一。它所用的绣线大多是较粗的加捻双股丝线，俗称衣线，故又称衣线绣。

Lu Embroidery

Lu Embroidery is a traditional embroidery form of the Han nationality unique to Shandong area. As one of the eight most famous embroidery forms in China, it is also the oldest one recorded in historical documents. The embroidery is not, merely practical for the making of clothes but also for appreciation of its art and craft.

济南面塑

俗称捏面人。它以糯米面为主料,调入不同色彩的颜料和防腐剂,用手指和简单工具小刀、小篦子、竹针等,塑造各种栩栩如生的塑像,是中国汉族的一种传统民间艺术,至今已有 300 多年的历史。

Ji'nan Dough Modeling

Commonly known as dough figuring, this traditional handicraft of the Han nationality has a history of over 300 years. Pigments and preservatives are added into sticky rice powder to make dough. The craftsmen then make the colored dough into vivid figures, animals, and plants with their fingers and simple tools such as small knives and bamboo needles.

济南泥塑

作为民间工艺的济南泥塑起源可追溯到大汶口文化、龙山文化时期,是济南民间传统的一种雕塑工艺。泥塑艺术作为非物质文化遗产具有很高的艺术性,它蕴含着深厚和丰富的文化内涵。

Ji'nan Clay Figuring

As an intangible cultural heritage, the highly artistic Ji'nan Clay Figuring dates back to the era of Dawenkou Civilization and Longshan Civilization. This traditional art of sculpture has profound cultural deposits.

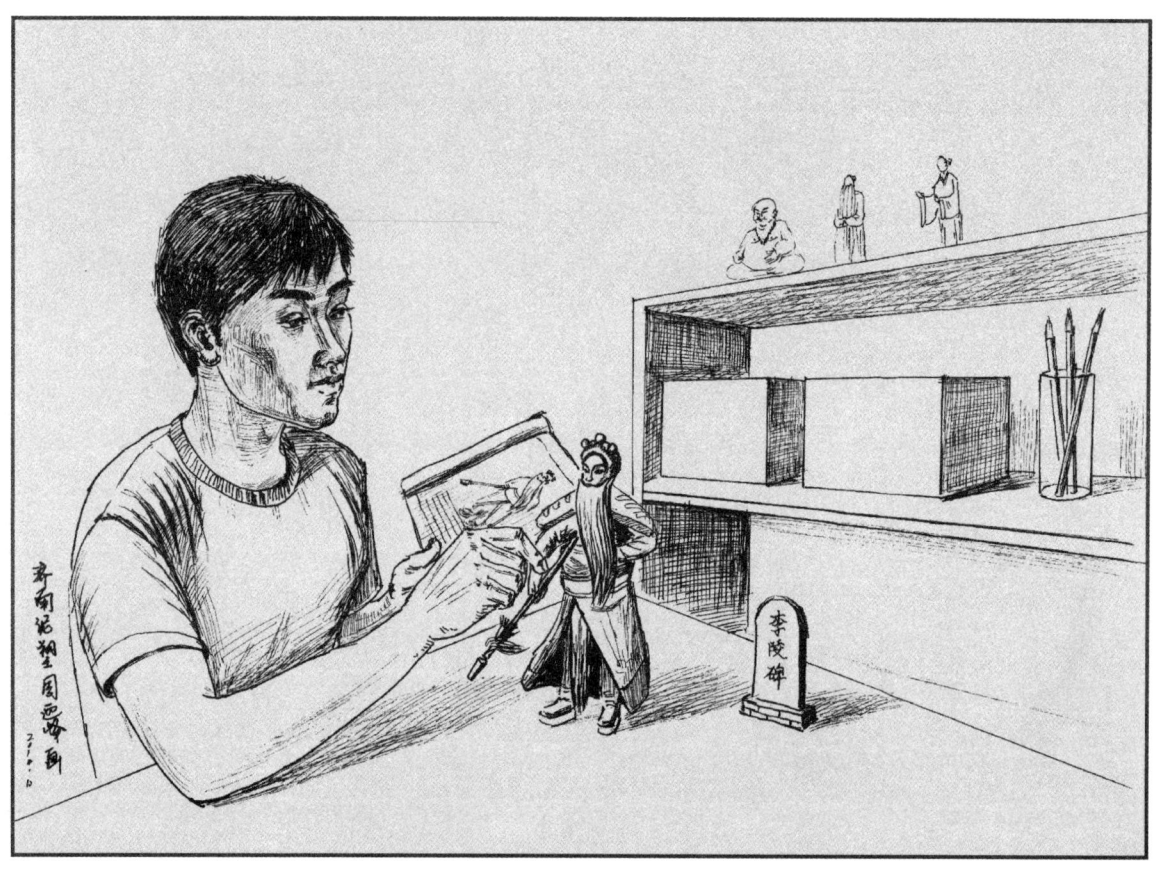

济南剪纸

　　剪纸艺术作为世界文化艺术中的一枝奇葩,一项非物质文化遗产,不仅为世界各国所喜爱,而且已发展成为国际交往中一门影响广泛的艺术。济南作为省会城市,自古就是齐鲁文化的交汇点,剪纸艺术深深融汇在这座历史文化名城中。

Ji'nan Papercutting

Papercutting, as its name suggests, is a folk art form that artists cut different patterns on the paper with scissors or graver to wish for blessings or drive out evil spirits. Ji'nan Papercutting combines the delicacy of the papercutting in southern China and the boldness of that in northern China.

侯氏社火脸谱

　　侯氏社火脸谱是山东省的汉族传统手工艺术珍品，被誉为济南一绝。始于清嘉庆二十五年（1820年），由老济南府历城郡的老先生"脸谱侯"制作，脸谱主要有山东济南、泰安当地汉族民间崇尚的保护神等。侯氏社火脸谱不仅仅是纯手工制作，而且传承了浓郁的齐鲁文化。

The Hou's Club Fire Facial Mask

unique treasure of the traditional handwork in Ji'nan, the Hou's Club Fire Facial Mask started in 1820 by the old artisan Hou the Facial Mask in Licheng Jun of Ji'nan. The facial masks mostly portray the patron saints worshiped by the Han nationalities in Ji'nan and Tai'an. The Hou's Facial Masks are purely handmade with the rich cultural heritage of the Shandong area.

葫芦雕刻

　　葫芦雕是既非单纯的范制,也非单纯的雕刻,而是将范制、雕刻、火绘、拼接组合融为一体,成为一门综合的葫芦器工艺,分为葫芦雕和刻葫芦和烫画。

Calabash Engraving

Characters or pictures are engraved in calabash to fashion it into a piece of artwork. There are three forms: calabash engraving, carving and pyrography.

周氏兔子王

周氏兔子王,取济南黄河滩边的黄河细泥土——干子土为原料,有大红袍、站王、坐虎、坐墩等十多个传统造型。周氏兔子王的手艺传到周秉生,已经是第四代。

The Zhou's Rabbit Clay Figuring

The Zhou's Rabbit Clay Figuring uses the fine clay from the shoal of the Yellow River to form rabbits of different shapes. There are over a dozen different traditional models, such as rabbit in red robe, standing rabbit king, sitting rabbit and crouching rabbit, etc. Zhou Bingsheng is the fourth-generation inheritor of the craftsmanship.

绣球灯

起源于济南市长清区境内的赵营村，是以手龙和绣球灯为道具，以武术和民艺相结合的一种舞蹈艺术形式。

Silk Ball Lantern Dance

Originated from Zhaoying Village in Changqing District, Ji'nan, the Silk Ball Lantern Dance is an art of folk dance combining Kongfu and folk artwork. Dancers hold dragon lanterns and silk ball lanterns while dancing.

> 章丘铁匠

　　起源于明未清初，章丘是"铁匠之乡"，历史悠久。20世纪50年代初统计，章丘境内人口为73万，约有38万人以打铁养家糊口。

Blacksmith in Zhangqiu

Zhangqiu has been the home of blacksmiths since the late Ming dynasty (1368-1644) and early Qing dynasty (1644-1911). Statistics in the early 1950s showed that approximately 380,000 of the 730,000 citizens in Zhangqiu made their livings as blacksmiths.

> 千佛山庙会

千佛山庙会是集祭祀、歌舞、文娱于一体的汉族民俗活动，在庙会上表演杂技、马戏、歌舞等，人流如潮，热闹非凡。它寄托了汉族劳动人民一种祛邪、避灾、祈福的美好愿望。

Temple Fair on Mount Qianfo
Temple Fair on Mount Qianfo is a folk activity of the Han nationality combining sacrifice, singing, dancing and other cultural activities. Starting from the Yuan dynasty (1206-1368), People climb Mount Qianfo and appreciate chrysanthemum blossoms on "Chrysanthemum Appreciation Rock" during the Double Ninth Festival.

宏济堂传统中药

　　宏济堂，始创于清光绪三十三年（1907年），在百年的改革发展中，传承了宏济堂的传统优秀文化。2008年宏济堂传统中药文化入选济南市第二批非物质文化遗产名录。

Hongjitang Traditional Chinese Medicine

Founded in 1907, the culture of Hongjitang traditional Chinese medicine has passed down from generation to generation for over 100 years.

大观园晨光茶社

大观园晨光茶社是著名相声大师孙少林先生与他的恩师李寿增先生联合大观园，在1943年一起创办的一处专门用来从事曲艺、相声表演的场所，茶社坐落在大观园商场东门内，是济南相声兴盛的标志。2007年，晨光相声大会被评为济南非物质文化遗产。

Chenguang Tea House in Daguanyuan Mall

In 1943, Mr. Sun Shaolin, a famous cross-talk artist, and his teacher Li Shouzeng joined with Daguanyuan Mall to found the Chenguang Teahouse for the performance of cross-talk and other folk arts. The teahouse is located inside the east gate of Daguanyuan Mall and is a landmark for the popularity of Ji'nan cross-talk.

明湖采藕

大明湖收藕基本靠"踩"。踩藕人身穿不透水的连身牛皮衣，用脚探索水下的藕枝，在藕节处用力一踩，用脚尖把藕瓜挑出水，捞一把黑泥涂在断口，再摇着小船将藕收集起来。

Lotus Root Harvest in Daming Lake

The lotus root harvest in Daming Lake is mostly dependant on "stepping". The lotus root collectors in water-proof one-piece cattlehide suit grope in the water with their feet for the lotus roots and step hard on the joint, then pick up the root with the tiptoe, smear some black mud on the fracture and put the root on a small boat.

放河灯

又称放荷灯，是一种汉族的民间祭祀及宗教活动，用以表达对逝去亲人的悼念，对活着的人们的祝福。每到特定日子，济南市民在就会在护城河放河灯祈福求平安。

Floating River Lanterns

Also called Floating Lotus Lanterns, it is a folk religious activity among the Han nationalities to mourn for the lost relatives and bless the surviving ones. Ji'nan citizens will float lanterns in the city moat to wish for peace on a particular day.

> 章丘芯子

　　章丘芯子是扮玩活动中的一种汉族民间艺术形式，因为酷似蜡烛台上的灯芯而得名。章丘芯子起源于明代，是受颠轿的启迪而来。芯子经过几代民间艺人的创造与革新，具有较高的观赏性和艺术性，颇受观众喜爱。

Zhangqiu Xinzi

Originated from the Ming Dynasty (1368-1644), Xinzi is a form of folk arts in the Han nationalities. Children dressed as heavenly gods dance on a platform or square table, which looks like the candlewick on. That's how the art form got its name. (In Chinese, Xinzi means wick.) It reflects the laboring people's longing for a better life.

> 形意拳

　　形意拳，又称心意六合拳，汉族传统拳术之一，与太极拳、八卦掌齐名，同属三大内家拳。济南形意拳现已被山东省政府收录到省级非物质文化遗产名录，作为非物质文化遗产，将受到保护。

Xingyi Chinese Boxing

Xingyi Chinese Boxing, also known as Xinyi Liuhe Boxing, is one of the traditional Chinese boxing forms equally famous with Tai Chi boxing and Eight Diagrams Palm. Now it has been listed as the Provincial Intangible Cultural Heritage by Shandong provincial government.

太平拳

太平拳是萌发与流传于山东平阴的一个具有百年历史的古老拳种，它源流有序，技法清晰，自成体系，已入选山东省非物质文化遗产名单。太平拳主要包括：基本功、拳术套路、器械套路、对练套路、实战技术、硬功功法、轻功功法等内容。

Taiping Chinese Boxing

Originating from Shandong Pingyin during the reign of Qing Emperor Kangxi (1662-1722), Taiping Chinese boxing is a century-old form of Chinese boxing with distinct features and a system of its own.